IN MY OWN RHYME

Susan North

ARTHUR H. STOCKWELL LTD
Torrs Park, Ilfracombe, Devon, EX34 8BA
Established 1898
www.ahstockwell.co.uk

© *Susan North, 2022*
First published in Great Britain, 2022

The moral rights of the author have been asserted.

*All rights reserved.
No part of this publication may be reproduced
or transmitted in any form or by any means,
electronic or mechanical, including photocopy,
recording, or any information storage and
retrieval system, without permission
in writing from the copyright holder.*

*British Library Cataloguing-in-Publication Data.
A catalogue record for this book is available
from the British Library.*

ISBN 978-0-7223-5140-6
*Printed in Great Britain by
Arthur H. Stockwell Ltd
Torrs Park   Ilfracombe
Devon EX34 8BA*

Some funny, others heartfelt. But most of all, every single one genuine and sincere.

1

Tell me how you feel, is your love for real?
If you don't talk, I'll take a walk.
There'll be a riot, if you stay quiet.
Say something, won't you please.
I'm begging on my knees.
For a parrot that's supposed to say a lot.
I've got one, who'd rather not.

2

Don't look back and regret the things you didn't do.
Who cares about the past when the future is waiting for you?
Take opportunities that come your way.
Not think, I'll leave it for another day.
You've one life, so live it to the fullest.
Because if you don't, your life will be the dullest.

3

The autumn leaves upon the trees,
Shades of red, gold and brown, how they astound!
If it's colder, I don't care, I've plenty of coats to wear.
And I simply love being wrapped up in hat, scarf and gloves.
I love this season, for so many reasons.
Yes, I like the rest, but for me,
Autumn is the best.

4

"Dinner's ready," my hubby says.
So, I rush to my place.
He's cooked tonight, so I know it'll be alright.
His stews and casseroles are a treat,
Simply good enough to eat.
I get stuck into my meal, and do so with such zeal.
This is fine, it's just right.
What my hubby cooked tonight.

5

I've just stepped back in time and guess what I find,
I'm writing poems and rhymes.
Maybe I didn't see that this was meant to be for me.
Has it always been there, this thing I can share?
It's what I'm going to pursue for myself, and all of you.

6

Music is my friend!
Am I going round the bend?
Then a song comes on, and I sing along.
There's nothing like a record to stop you getting bored.
Lifts your spirits high, you feel you could fly.
Well, I'm telling you there's no doubt.
Music is what it's all about.

7

Oh, my aching knees!
I'm a museum piece.
I'd beg for a new pair of legs.
For goodness' sake, it seems I will ache.
No matter how many lotions or potions or creams.
It doesn't ease.
So please, I say to my knees and legs, don't make me frown.
Every time I rise from my chair or sit down.

8

The scent of a rose.
Sweet perfume to my nose.
This perfect flower, I could look at for hours.
A bloom like no other, if no other flowers, I wouldn't bother.
Because the rose, to me, is perfection, and the colours – what a selection.
But personally, the colour for me has got to be the red.

9

Get on living the life you have.
Don't try to outdo others, be brave.
Do your own thing, sing or shout.
That's what it's all about.
You came into this world with nowt.
So what if you do the same when you go out.

10

Been to visit Aunty May.
I told her I couldn't stay.
Not too long anyway.
Because every time I sit down her Great Dane comes bounding around.
He's not particular where he lays.
The bloomin' mutt, usually on my foot.
Well, I got up at last to save my tootsie being put in a cast.
Bid Aunty May goodbye as that big brute looked me in the eye.

11

You can be exactly what you want to be.
That is clear to me now, yes, I see.
Just believe in your own ability.
Then look at the possibilities.
It's never too late, the rewards will be great.
So go on, do it, don't leave it too late.

12

I looked in the mirror, and to my horror
I looked a fright!
Too many beers last night.
The evidence is there.
Eight empty bottles beside my chair.
Well, if this is how it's going to be after a few drinks,
I'll stick to water, I think.

13

On a bus trip today,
The guy with his wife, had plenty to say.
Poor woman couldn't get a word in, he was making such a din.
He'd been here and he'd been there,
Goodness, he'd been everywhere.
I wouldn't care, but he was talking so loud,
His voice would have been heard in a crowd.
How come every time I travel somewhere,
There's someone to spoil the journey, and I wish I wasn't there.

14

Walking along the sand in my own world.
With no demands.
Yes, this is calming, most charming.
What is it about the sea
Makes you feel free?
In tune with myself, nobody else.
The sand, sky and sea, they're perfect to me.
Better than therapy.
Out go the stresses and strains, nothing remains
But you, refreshed and anew.

15

I was walking down the street, heard the pitter-patter of little feet.
It's the girl from next door bless her, she's only four.
She started school on Monday, she'd run up to me to say.
Sally's little jumper hitched so high; goodness knows why.
Her socks were down to the ground, shoelaces undone.
Gosh I bet she'd had some fun.
Well, I had to smile at her mum.

16

It's no surprise, when I look into your eyes,
The love that I see, is especially for me.
That look I've seen over the years,
Has allayed my fears, abated my tears.
I'm so grateful that you're near.
So, look into my eyes, and you won't be surprised
To see the love that burns for you, in return.

17

On the quayside, am I.
Watching the boats go by.
So tranquil a scene.
I lean on the rail, as the bright sails flap in the breeze.
My senses are teased.
I often stand here, there's a pub across there.
So, I have a glass of beer.
I may have a snack later on, when the boats have gone.
But, at the moment, I'm content to stand here.
Watch the world passing by, in front of my eyes.

18

How long have I known Joe, from next door?
I'm not sure.
Must be a while.
How come I've never noticed how gorgeous he looks
When he smiles?
Until a couple of days ago, out of the blue he says,
"Would you like to go out to a show?"
I looked absurd, as I was stuck for words.
That's not like me, I'm normally gobby, you see.
But finally, needless to say
I smiled back, and said "OK".

19

Since you passed away,
Each day,
I just amble away, I have to say.
No particular plan
For the day ahead.
I should stay in bed.
Life's lost its shine, it used to be fine.
It'll take some time
To get used to being alone, with no other at home.
I just hope and pray, that someday
The happiness I lack, will come back.

20

Your warm breath on my face.
I'm in your embrace.
Here I belong, in your arms so strong.
I look up to your face, and I know this is the only place
Where I'll feel safe.

21

If the skies had been blue that day,
Would you have gone away?
If the sun had shone, upon your face,
Would you still be here, in this place?
But, it's no good me going over and over in my head.
You wanted to be somewhere else instead
And that somewhere
Wasn't with me.

22

I'm on the outside, looking in.
Sometimes feel I can't win.
All alone, on my own.
If anyone cared, they'd be there.
But they stare!
What do they see?
Are they looking at me?
Or am I a ghost to them all?
I call!!
Does anyone hear?
The answer's no, I fear.
So I'll continue to look, to stare.
Till someone notices me there.

23

Standing here by the tree,
Where you and me stood, many years before.
I wasn't sure, at the time,
But you wanted to be mine.
To have a future together, to part, never.
Now, I stand here alone, and I am missing you so,
As you passed away, on this very day, one year ago.

24

He could barely talk,
But when we went for a walk,
He knew all the car names; it was always the same.
Under two years old, was he, our Lee.
People in the street, everyone we used to meet
Were impressed with this little tot, who before he was two
Knew such a lot.

25

Better not tarry,
Have a date with Larry.
Mustn't be late, as he won't wait.
Gotta be prompt, or he'll get the hump.
I'll wager, in another life
He was a sergeant major.

26

I glance up from my book, I'm entranced.
The glare of the sun shines upon your favourite armchair.
You used to love to sit there, sun shining on your handsome face.
That was your place, your space.
But since you passed away, my only comfort, I have to say,
Is to glance over to your chair, on a day like today
And make believe you're still there.

27

A new day has dawned, another morning.
Things that were making me sad yesterday, have now gone.
There's a new day to look upon.
Like leaves from the trees, in the breeze
Bad times have blown away.

28

The river steadily flows, and goodness knows,
How many boats go past, wish this moment could last.
On the bank, we've had a perfect day, passing time away.
A picnic lunch, lots of goodies to munch.
Better make the most of the rest of this summer afternoon.
It'll be over all too soon.

29

We share a home, but I may as well be alone.
You're quiet all the time.
Never a word from you.
What should I do?
I've tried to speak, but silence.
I take offence.
All you're bothered about is getting your food and drink.
What am I supposed to think?
But what can I expect, oh and did I neglect to tell you
I was talking about my parrot Lou?

30

Often, I just sit and stare,
Into some space over there.
Wish I didn't sometimes, as cobwebs are on the blinds.
I can tell, 'cause when the sun shines through
That's when I do.
But, hey ho, that's the way it goes.
I'm no slave to housework, and it shows.

31

We sit on the balcony, me and you.
This sweet cottage, complete with sea view.
The hustle and bustle left behind.
Here we find we're content.
This place was heaven sent, for us two, it was meant.

32

There's me, I'm carefree, and why shouldn't I be?
I see every sight and hear every sound.
I'm bound to be happy.
To feel this way on the brightest of days.
With the bluest of skies, it's no surprise.

33

Why didn't I say the words that were needed?
Maybe then, we would have succeeded.
But no, I didn't talk and so you walked.
Only myself to blame, it hurts all the same.

34

Well, you made it to the top, now what?
At the expense of your family,
Wouldn't you agree, the ones at home you never see?
Babies Jack and Michael and me.
Where would you be,
Without the sacrifices that we made?
My nights alone at home,
Children crying, there's no denying,
We sacrificed our lives for you to be a success.
Now we're in a mess.

35

Fly high, my pretty white bird.
Fly as high up above, my sweet dove,
As your wings will take you.
For my sake, do, as I'm depending on you
To break through the clouds
That shroud my love from view.

36

Could I have guessed, that day,
As you walked through the door,
That would be the last time I would see you?
If only I knew.
I could have said much more.
But I couldn't have known.
You left me alone.
My darling pet cat, whom I'd had since a kitten.
Now you've gone missing.

37

I can't wait, for my date.
Will he be late?
Who knows, only met him last week.
My anxiety grows.
I feel weak.
What to wear, the red or black dress?
Or even the silver, as it sparkles in the darkness?
Oh, what am I on about?
My mind's all over the place.
My heart's beginning to race.

38

So fed up of waiting, phone at my ear,
For someone to appear on the end of the line.
To talk to anybody, would be fine.
It wouldn't be so bad, I wouldn't get so mad.
But I forget the reason for calling.
It's appalling.
Whatever happened to the old days
When you could pick up the phone
And someone answered straight away?

39

Reflecting, looking back, our life together.
The heartache we've had to weather.
But we've done this between us two.
Yes, me and you.
And forever, will continue.

40

Those trees over there, in the distance,
Where we stood at the beginning of our romance.
You looked into my eyes,
And I espied the same love and affection from you,
That I felt for you too.

I do hope you've enjoyed reading a selection of my poems. I hadn't done any writing before, but enjoyed English at school. But, anyway, I think this all came about because of our life-changing experience back in 2011. To cut a long story short, my husband very nearly died, as his heart was blocked, that is, the aortic artery was exploding inside him, due to a genetic condition. Then, soon after, one of my nephews committed suicide, which, again was heartbreaking. So, since then, the only way to pour out my feelings is through writing poetry.

Susan North